MW01502854

Rhythmic Expressions
The Next Dimension

An Edgar Folks Original
By
Edgar A. Folks

Published by Folks Development, LLC
Printed in the U.S.A.

For bookings or orders, contact:
Edgar A. Folks
E-mail: eaf5454@gmail.com
Phone: 412.224.0605

Library of Congress Control Number: 1-2163805771
Reference Id: 1-ZS9VAI

ISBN-13: 978-1508579373
ISBN-10:1508579377

Book Cover Assistance
Christopher Tally Sr.
Publishing, Layout, Design, & Distribution
Edgar Folks
Folks Development LLC and

Rhythmic Expressions
The Next Dimension

An Edgar Folks Original
By
Edgar A. Folks

Table of Contents

Acknowledgements
Introduction

"One" Pillow Talk

"Two" The Truth

"Three" When Love Hurts

Acknowledgements

To my legacy: Ethan, Destiny, Aaron, and Edgar
Folks:
There are no limitations to your dreams. It is my
hope and prayer that your accomplishments are
limitless.

To: Michelle Hornsby, Sharon Vescera and Dianne
W. Carter
Thank you for all your help and support.

Last, but first, Jesus, the Christ, my Lord and
Savior,
THANK YOU!

Introduction

The man has taken off the mask and exposed his blind spots to give you "Rhythmic Expressions the Next Dimension". Come fill the deep expressions of a man's evolution through life as well as his continuous growth and development moving en-route to the next dimension. Explore through his lens of love, being loved, and many other lessons learned. You will definitely enhance your knowledge of mankind after Rhythmic Expressions the Next Dimension.

Pillow Talk

Loves a beautiful thing, but sometimes it stings,
I will always pursue it whatever it takes,
because making love is great, wouldn't you
agree? So, I dedicated this chapter and verse to
the things I love the most and that's love, loving,
and making love. Please enjoy

Yes to You

Rejuvenation of my heart was a start, and then you massaged my mind redefining all my quality time. Next, you let my love infiltrate your inner most parts of that passionate heart, and moving forward we will continuously press rewind keeping this Love on the forefront of our minds. Staying into one another saying no to any others because I have that love for you that's living, it's like a gift that's forever giving.

Next Dimension

When you find the one person who captures all your humanity keep them for eternity

Separating Thoughts

I'm consistently thinking of you; hopefully you're reciprocating those thoughts of me too. Baby, I know love is blind but my heart doesn't lie. Lately, my eyes swell with tears for the fear of you saying bye, due to you no longer wanting to be mine. I hoped and prayed that we could be together forever. Nevertheless, I will respect your wishes and stay away, but optimistically wishing this isn't our reality.

Next Dimension

Reality is the conclusion of facts and wishful thinking is predicting of random acts.

One more Time

Baby, quality time is what I have to share, your
needs I'm willing to bare, and for your heart I have
an abundance of cares. So, I'm asking for the last
time, are you going to be mine? For my love is
deep, but without you I'll still be complete. If the
answer is no the tears may flow, but they'll dry
and I'll say goodbye.

Next Dimension

Goodbye may not be defined as forever, but time
has a beginning and end date.

Greatest Design

God's greatest design is a Woman for she is so divine. With her beautiful full wool like hair, silky caramel skin, pink lips, proportionate hips, and her two tone nips. Please don't ignore her sensuous silhouette for that would be a big regret. Personally, I like a nice behind. Thank you Lord for keeping that in mind, I must confess woman are blessed and also equipped to give birth to the next generation of this earth. Last, but not least, the woman's intimate thing is any straight man's dream for I can't get enough of her exquisite touch.

Next Dimension

The world is filled with greatness. Nevertheless, greatness doesn't compare to a woman to whom I want to become one with.

Use

I want you to be the one to have my daughter or
son, and my wife for life, as well as the love we
share as our devotion of emotions. If by chance,
we ever get sick sexual healing will do the trick. I
want my kiss to only taste your lips and if we're
ever apart you'll have the only key to my heart.
The radiance from our affection flows and the
reflection glows, so you're not hard to miss and I'll
forever find you with this kiss

Next Dimension

When your soulmate is sharing their heart it is
imperative that you're attentive

Never

Never had anybody quite like you, a love so great,
you're the girl of my world for you unleashed all
the chains from my brain. Now, I incorporate you
in all I do for we are united as one. With this love
we can restrain any pain and live a purpose filled
life as husband and wife.

Next Dimension

Love will conquer all.

No Body

One of a kind, a touch of infinity within time, for you have the blueprint into my mind. All my fantasies are assigned to your intricacies. For loving you is my destiny. This sounds strange, but I'm engaged to the point of being enslaved to your aroma, for when you're around I drift into a functioning coma. I'll never be the same for your love changed the game

Next Dimension

When love is controlling your body, soul and mind, it is what it is!

Companionship

Please accompany me continuously flowing in love and adoration. Baby, equanimity is my gifted ability to disseminate it through our future. I have an obsession for your presence for I want to wrap my hands around your waist; all the while caressing your body in a steady pace for this foreplay is a scheduled date each time we mate. If you have any need, fulfillment will be my deed. So sit back and enjoy. I guarantee it will be better than your toys. Just say yes, and I'll take your body through a quest nice and slow as we let the evening flow.

Next Dimension

Having a spouse on the same accord is a beautiful situation.

True Confessions

She said to me "yeah you have gifts, but you are also a nymph and you want to do me any chance you get". My reply was, "I agree that's a big segment of my abilities and I believe you're blessed because your body and mind is fulfilled all the time. If I was you I wouldn't complain for you never say no and after we finish I see that glow as you flow deep into sleep. For that's when I know my job is complete. "then she said, "I agree, now come over here and make love to me!"

Next Dimension

Sometimes words are said just to be heard.

Righteous

If all was right we will wait until we're wed before making love instead. If all was right you will be my wife for my entire life. If all was right there would be no strive and purpose would define my life. If all was right my mind wouldn't take flight and there would be no need to walk towards the light. If all was right there would be no need for darkness, evening, nor night, because the sun would permanently shine bright. Yes if all was right

Next Dimension

It's great to dream and hope those dreams integrate into reality.

Good Things come with Time

Baby, if I'm not on your mind; just give it time, for
I assigned all of me to make our relationship the
ultimate in unity and intimacy. All I've done is
directly focused on making you the one to
stimulate me in every way as well as taking my
body down in your lavish ways. Within that vain
the feeling is the same. Whatever your need I will
fulfill and exceed with enjoyment and moist fun.
So, whatever it takes to receive your time as mine
will be just fine.

Next Dimension

Confidence could be the key ingredient to
capturing the love of another.

Imaginations

Eventually, fantasies over take my reality then I'm wishful thinking of things we have never done but consistently hoping that we could become one. I have visions of my love keeping you in a time of need, listening to your every thought and making those thoughts my inspiration, not to control but console. Our souls will be so in touch when you sneeze I will feel it as I breathe

Next Dimension

When you love a person unconditionally you hope they reciprocate that love.

A Love Story

The day we met I will never forget for I regret the past time I explored only to find your love is divine. You're a dream come true, for that I thank God for a blessing dressed in flesh and that defines you.

Next Dimension

Finding true love is a possibility.

Much Love

That queen was in my grasp, but our time has passed. I'm talking about the love I once had. It took me to a place where it's neither time nor space, but fallacy brought me back to reality of me infinitely loving the queen of my dreams.

Next Dimension

Nurture the love you have, because it can become the love you once had.

Dreaming of You

Time is never better spent bonding with you. When you're not home my mind roams back to our intimate connections and those desires I'm continuously projecting visions of you and I. Then, when you come back we turn those fantasies into realities one after another. I love your participation for without you there's no gratification.

Next Dimension

The desire of your spouse is appropriate.

Full Disclosure

May I walk with you hand in hand yearning to star in your fantasy? I'm thankful for the opportunity to converse with you. If by chance, can we have a meal or two and my hope will permanently be your dessert. I will caress your heart with all my pleasure, no pain, much sunshine and minimum rain. The only thing I want to reinforce is me being loyal if I'm your only choice.

Next Dimension

Being trustworthy throughout a relationship will prolong the friendship.

Trigger a Notion

I just want to stimulate your thoughts, keeping the
conversation sharp and hoping you get a spark.
Then, wishfully thinking we become one with
fulfillment and fun saturating us with love and
devotion with this initial notion. We would be on a
quest to discover who loves the best. Whoever
wins will request a rematch and redo the loving
contest again and again. It will be our quest for the
other's best and never settling for less.

Next Dimension

Effective communication can open the entrance for
a sense of excitement.

For Granted

In past relationships I accepted what was disclosed. Now I have criteria and if you want to be more than acquaintances the prerequisite is to exceed my expectations. For the hour is late in this stage of life and I have no time designated for conflict or fights. So if I'm not your type of dude, that's cool because knowing up front saves time and energy.

Next Dimension

Lost time can't be redeemed.

Abundance

Love is for the giving, life is for the living baby I
have an abundance of both, so just know I want to
have your love, for chills run through my spine
when you come to mind therefore, I want to give
you all of my time.

Next Dimension

If you want love to flow, then you have to let your
love go in that direction.

Lasting Taste

I drifted into a memory of you, it felt so right just
us two in the dark filled with candle lights.
Blistering so bright your silhouette was delightful.
Then, I awoke and my heart was broke. It was like
a room full of toys to an adolescent boy. So, I want
to be where you are for my mind shifts back to you
and the things we used to do. Therefore, don't get it
twisted I'm forever missing it, I know what we had
is the past, but unlike a piece of gum that sweet
taste will never go away but stay with me.

Next Dimension

Memories are the art of fantasy because you can
recall past experiences and reenact that occasion.

Ecstasy

You took me there, so high I believed flying was a natural reaction implemented by our attraction, or was it my satisfaction of your intimate gratification? I have to admit I'm addicted to your love making. It put me to sleep to the point I need to cease for your pleasure points is a beast that forced me to release without restriction, but the ambition to restart again and again and then again.

Next Dimension

When the love making is the real deal you will come home on time and never miss a meal.

On my Mind

The times we shared was absent of tears as well as fear but much love my dear. All our concerns were forsaken and continuous love we were making three or four times countless nights for your body was so tight. My 7.5 fit just right! At times, I couldn't believe it was real the way you made me feel until you were gone with only thoughts on my mind to linger on.

Next Dimension

When reality evolves into memories that's a sign of the end of you and me

Tootsie roll

So sweet and beyond I'm talking about her ambience, the passing of her love is the only thing I fear. It's addictive as well as true each night her loving calls I answer like a romantic trace. I consistently dance to her intimate song all night long.

Next Dimension

Love is the greatest gift.

Searching

Most of my adult life I've been looking for a woman that I could call my wife abandon from deception, malice, or strife. I wanted to share my life and all I have to bare without restrictions or fear. All I ever wanted is a single love, so today I search and explore for that one; I will fly high and soar to find that one I can claim as my wife. So I'm searching! Do you want to be found?

Next Dimension

Searching and then finding that right person is part of the pleasure of love.

You Know Me

Baby, I'm well groomed. I bring pleasant smells to a room so don't dispute my display for you know you want to eat from my tray. I'm no trick, so you don't have to pay with cash but amongst other things you have to do to make this thing last. If you want a one night stand then I'm not your man for my plan is a life session with continuous lessons so join this team of purpose and dreams.

Next Dimension

It's a fine line between confidence and pride.

Okay

Baby, let me drift into your subconscious while
you read my mind. Let me kiss your heart as you
saturate my emotions, allowing me to infiltrate
your mind as you mold me like clay. Instruct me
how to love you while I facilitate your affections.

Next Dimension

Growth and development in a relationship is great
when partners enhance one another.

What's up?

Baby, I thirst for a sip for those juicy lips, and eventually a kiss between your hips. Matter fact, I demand a cup to consume it all up, excuse me for the greed, but your body's calling me and I must answer the need.

Next Dimension

Gratifying your spouse will bring satisfaction to your home.

Real Rap

Baby, your beauty is divine, the body is well designed and if you could be so kind to let me invest in your mind, for I would download all my forget-me-nots in your thoughts until I capture your heart.

Next Dimension

Your presentation will get you into the door. Character along with skills will get you promoted.

Winter Seasons

Chilly times are bittersweet. It's a season to
cuddle, eat and give that love one a special treat.
Yes, it's cold and just right for producing babies
by moon light. So, enjoy one another as well as the
intimate bliss for love travels through the bitter air
kissing away fears and freezing all tears. I'm
humbled by the cheer for the holidays are near.

Next Dimension

Cold weather can warm the heart.

What I Want

Baby, lets combine our hearts, that'll be our initial start to a bond that we'll never depart. Let's practice love as a perfected art and then we project it for all to see, me loving you and you loving me forever and a day

Next Dimension

If you want your relationship to go to the next dimension communication is the tool.

Reunited

All things being equal you and I should make a sequel, and to start I want to kiss your heart. I'm making a commitment that we will never depart again for I want to love you to no end. Sweetheart, just say, "Yes" and I'll promise to give you my best!

Next Dimension

Petitioning for what you want isn't a bad thing.

Protected

Time and time again my love was rejected now my
heart stays protected. So, if you want to share in
my love you have to be sincere. Please, if you
enjoy lying, there's no need for applying. You will
be awarded a key for true love and humility.

Next Dimension

Be up front with your demands and qualifications
before you give the gifts and benefits.

True Confession

This is for the things I should've done but didn't.
Here's for all the things I should've said, but
couldn't. This is for the feelings I felt, but didn't
filter them within your mind, and this is for the
times I gave you less than my best. Today, I'm
going to start caressing your mind as well as
stimulation your spine each time we're together. It
will be better than our last encounter, satisfaction
guaranteed, regrets you will never need for my
love runs deep. I will admire you until infinity
expands its reach.

Next Dimension

When you demonstrated truth you will receive
sincerity in return.

No one else

Silky and smooth my lungs collapse each time you move for there's no one like you. Baby, loving you will be class personified wherever you want to go I will be your ride for no one else will I choose because you are you and the love inside me will always be your jewels.

Next Dimension

When you love a person even death can't change those feelings.

Absolute

Your love is so sweet and absolutely unique that we must make love the whole valentine's week. For this will guarantee that you're feeling me in every way as well as with no restrictions and minimum intermissions. Until you validate me as your mate.

Next Dimension

Valentine's Day is my favorite holiday.

Love Bandit

Baby, you stole it with a kiss and a twist of those hips therefore, you are a master extortionist. You took my love and vowed to never let it go and you made my house a happy home.

Next Dimension

Sometimes, you have to talk the love language before you make the love.

2 sessions into 1

The initial session begins with rotating lickings and additional kissing. The tongue is a beautiful thing, as I do wondrous things that bring reality to your dreams. Then we do it in a formal motion until you release your love potion flowing in every direction as you are erupting with erotic sensations. You thought that was the end but after a brief intermission the second session begins co-starring 7.5 interceding for you in a horizontal and vertical motion until an accelerating explosion, after a coma induced sleep begins.

Next Dimension

When your spouse surprises you it brings joy to the occasion.

Rejection

You reject my love like it's really bad, but this is something you never gave a chance. Hopefully, you enjoy being happy versus sad and warm in the arms of a real man. If this is so let me attempt to make you glow, I promise to give you my best and for you I aim to impress!

Next Dimension

I'm hoping for a mutual reaction to my initial attraction.

Dream Date

This one is dedicated to you. You know who you are. It's no longer a fantasy, but my star, not to be referred to as a date, but my future soulmate. Please come unto me for I need your touch and so much more because you are loved and adored.

Next Dimension

At some point in time you have to express your true intentions

Real Talk

I have this particular set of skills that will seal our deal so you can anticipate your fate. Therefore, your future looks great as my mate. I want you to participate in our thing as equals. I have confidence there will be no sequels. I will continuously love you for no particular reason as well as grow and develop in all our seasons.

Next Dimension

Love is a beautiful thing

Why Not

An initial bubble bath will lead to a path of serenity for you and me. Then in more ways than one baby, let's have fun. Some laughter with jokes, and massaging of those toes one by one within a pleasure filled night with slow music and for your appetite, breakfast in bed by daylight. These types of eventful nights will keep our current situation right.

Next Dimension

Keep the relationship growing with the juices of love continuously flowing

Attraction

Attraction is an emotion that doesn't need interaction. Nevertheless, the body needs satisfaction to confirm the urge. The mind wonders and attempts to turn that thought into reality. That's when your advances are either approved or denied by the person you have in mind

Next Dimension

Take a chance in the name of romance.

Body Talk

When I look in your tan eyes they said hi. Then, I heard those perky lips to my surprise saying give me a kiss. Next, I read those proportionate hips asking me to escort you on a trip to wonders and bliss, that's when our minds identified that this love is unified. Discovering this new form of communication, I anticipate something great when we get together tonight at eight, so make the body talk clever because I'm ready for whatever! Therefore, no restraints, let's be free to fulfill all our needs, pull out all the stops to let our bodies talk.

Next Dimension

Intimacy is better than silver and gold when needed.

Together

I want to be sure that you can endure my imperfections, as well as bringing your supremacy to my inferiority. Sweetheart, with your lead we can evolve towards the direction of perfection, not all at once but together we can grow so much!!!

Next Dimension

Humility in a relationship can enhance your fellowship.

When I Part

It breaks my heart that I have to part for my escort
has come and life on earth is done. I did my best to
pass every test, and granted many request. I'm
requested to go beyond for I sang my final song
hopefully, a strong legacy to carry on. My brand
rolled the tide, for I tried to minimize my pride.
Nevertheless, I lived in stride always with my faith
in God as my guide. Good bye

Next Dimension

My obituary

Sweet Talk

Baby, all is right with me, but I'm hoping for a
night of intimacy. I believe our connection will
produce life and I have so much love for you that I
can cut it with a knife. The feelings for you will
cease to end, for our legacy together has officially
started, therefore, killing, stealing, and being
unfulfilling has officially departed. The universe is
ours and the Lord has blessed you with this star,
that's shining bright so just say, "yes" and I'll turn
you out until we both scream and shout.

Next Dimension

Expressing yourself can be effective
communication.

Kisses

There's nothing better than getting those kisses from your misses, but don't get it twisted. They're more than kisses but infinite wishes of things to come. For those luscious kisses is a prelude to fun of our union as one. So, now you know my love flows when I get those kisses from my misses.

Next Dimension

Kissing can initiate a saturation of love making.

7.5

When I make love I work the angles, so don't ask me to cease for that brings out that beast. Therefore, stick to the plan and take it like a woman. It's never meant for you to weep when I go deep, but keeping it in strive when working with this 7.5. It's good but don't think of it as a snack for 7.5 has been known to attack, so face it head on in different directions for maximum pleasure, assuring the duration of love making.

Next Dimension

Love making is better when each party's movements are together.

Original Lady

I love the dark covering you wear. Don't you dare try to make it fair, that shapely behind, intelligent mind, juicy lips, fulfilling hips. Please don't forget the two tone nips that nurtured this earth at its birth. Sweetheart, you're fine and I love you with all my heart, soul, and mind. I know your self-esteem is a little tart, because you had it rough from the start, but God loves you with all his heart.

Next Dimension

Beauty is a component of blackness.

Get it done

I want to assist you with this kiss wherever for maximum pleasure and whenever. Just submit your request! If we keep this pace you will have our seed, wouldn't you agree, a direct reflection of us loving one another. An initial kiss will be replicated and the love we make will continuously be duplicated to no end.

Next Dimension

Love making is the initial process of bringing forth a new creation.

Confidence

Who do you think you're fooling? I know you want me as much as I want you. Let's stop talking, and remove these clothes until we see our fleshly tones, then I will escort you to the erogenous zone. Sweetheart, you're fearfully and wonderfully designed as well as owning space in my mind.

Next Dimension

Many say confidence is alluring to the touch.

Free Style

Baby, I don't care if you jumped off the moon into the sun. You're still the one for me, for the love we share is spread freely with our intimacy. We are one in unity, just you and I, keeping it steadily and freely doing one another as we please.

Next Dimension

An uninhabited love is a love with no restraints.

Exploration

What I have in store is always and forevermore the exploration of intimate satisfaction with minimal distractions, because the door will be closed to those who block when we start our body to body art, for its well designed with your body substituting as my canvas. As well as partnering with my bursting brush painting designs illustrating the fantasies of you in my mind.

Next Dimension

Exploring your spouse's body can be an exhilarating experience.

Pillow Talk

It's about the way you ride, the movement in your stride, and the walk that stimulates pillow talk. It's your grace all up in my face at a steady pace that will motivate me to perform those deeds that quiver your knees; it's all about the pillow talk. The way you move and the sensuous way you groove are major sparks of pillow talk.

Next Dimension

Stand by what you say and make it do what it do.

Part-Take In

Baby I'm steak and potatoes and could never be mistaken as a snack for I'll put soreness in your back and if you try to keep my pace then, sweat will continually race down your face. I make love on many levels for example: the mid-level is beat it up like a rebel. So pick and choose, because I usually make love to fit your mood.

Next Dimension

If you exceed the needs of your spouse you will have a happy house.

The Truth

Telling the truth is knowledge that needs to be spoken as well as heard. As you read this chapter reflect on your life and enjoy every moment we share.

My Tone

I write from the core that's why it's a breeze with these metaphors, love is my claim to fame, and when I sign my name there is no games. The ladies consistently request my resources, but of course, my wife is protecting, so the advances I'm rejecting. My rhythmic expressions are so good if writing was a crime then I'll be doing time, for I can't be contested. I know you heard of my fame writing lyrics is my game and yes Edgar Folks is my name

Next Dimension

Your gift will make room for you.

Legacy declined

They say the Apple doesn't fall too far from the tree, but I try my best to undo what was wrongfully prearranged for me. For my family tree was cruel it was borderline fulfilling the destiny of being a fool because of that I declined, and God gave me my own mind. Peace, love and some rage, but it's only acted out in managed stages. At a youthful stage I exhibited my rage to other fools my age but that was wrong and I learned as life evolved how to resolve conflict in productive and positive ways.

Next Dimension

Reinventing yourself will help with a productive life.

Greater or Less

There will always be people with greater or less
wisdom, knowledge and understanding. The key is
learning from the greater and encourage the less.

Next Dimension

This is one of the key factors to servant leadership.

I am Me

The Hill District is where I use to abide, now the north side is where I reside. My environment left a lasting impression but the Lord corrected all the suppression. Now, I have a focused life. I refuse to give depression space or time, because I believe God gave me the ability to accomplish whatever comes to mind, for it is the way I'm designed.

Next Dimension

Confidence is different than pride

Never been outlawed

I answer when you call, because that word nigga is still not outlawed. No matter how big or small it's an uncouth mindset that I regret because my ancestors paid the debt for the life we achieved and/or received. Nevertheless, with our own self-inflicted chains on our minds we will be left behind.

Next Dimension

The freedom of your mind can help mankind.

Stimulation of Thought

An initial stimulus of intuition can craft a response; integrated with educated advice will create a decision that's right. The streams of dreams romancing my heart will come true one by one, for it has begun in individual sessions. That's why I wrote "Teachable Moments" because I learned the lessons.

Next Dimension

Just ponder on it; it's deep!

Find Yourself

Before structuring and designing goals you have to find your self-worth and identity on this earth. Purpose is the initial rule to minimize becoming a fool. Then construct your life with the absence of fights or strife. Continue to develop from birth until you leave this earth. When at all possible keep peace with your fellow man and let all these domains be part of your brand.

Next Dimension

Core values are primary in defining character.

Validation

I recite numbers backwards. Nevertheless, I'm a
mathematician. Couldn't read fluently until the
12th grade nevertheless, I published and authored
five books. Validation comes from God for he
created me in his image. He's seen every tear, hurt,
and pain. My thoughts are in his mind and my
prayers are already predestined before time.
Eternity is where my God dwells and validation
begins and ends with him.

Next Dimension

Validation comes from the Lord.

My Son

You're missed, but never forgotten, gone for many moons but there's always hope. I will be with you very soon, bone of my bone and flesh of my flesh my son you're the best answer to my God given request.

Next Dimension

When a child is absent from your arms you hope and pray that everything's okay.

Tree

A tree is a symbol of me. I have infinite
possibilities, for growth and development is steep.
My foundation is deep and the endurance long
even when I'm not wrong, when the wind blows
my foundation shows for its grounded in loyalty
with stages of fidelity in something greater than
this earth where we were birthed. Nevertheless,
I'm different from the norm. It's love personified
in any storm

Next Dimension

The foundation of a thing is solid and grounded it
will withstand the demands of life's storms.

Why

People ask why I write in short story form. It's because I stay on message, but not stray from my blessings, and will deal with the aftermath. I'm blessed to do this thing by request as well as define all your trials and tests with a pen and pad. At the end of the day my writing will transform that sadness into gladness!

Next Dimension

I find enjoyment in blessing others.

Embrace the Climate

Seasons come and go, thunder will rumble,
lighting will glow, and rain will flow.
Nevertheless, all those trials will cease and in due
season there will be peace, so go through the
transition with strength and there's no need to be
tense. Endure the lessons you learn because those
stripes you will earn for living life is a blessing
with an abundance of testing.

Next Dimension

To have a great life one needs to embrace their
trials and tribulations.

Think Before You Act

You don't have to fear but please be aware of the skill set that I bare for it's very rare. You're about to make a life forsaking decision, this is a good time to use your intuition. Nevertheless that was the old me but I can switch back to that identity, and revisit that former man with the deadly hands. I believe you don't want this confrontation with me to be your fate, therefore chill like ice so you continue to live your life.

Next Dimension

Always be insightful and think before you act.

The Epitome of me

My personality is free flowing; mind roaming,
answers to questions knowing, and almost never
debating. A wonderful listener, poetic writer,
former fist fighter, and I really enjoy making love
lesson into an all-night session

Next Dimension

Enjoying life

Maturation of Brother Folks

Once I had many women to divide my mind. Now,
I'm married with children and that's how I share
my time. The past relationship was fun, but with
responsibility develops maturity and now I'm
married with children and life has officially begun.

Next Dimension

There is an appointed time to be a child, but when
you become an adult you have to develop those
childish ways.

Truism

What's up baby? I'm in that mode I've never grown
cold my soul will never be sold. Nevertheless, as I
age my wisdom will continuously unfold to
another dimension of truism. For I speak the truth
go look it up you'll find proof.

Next Dimension

The truth will always prevail.

Mid Son

Son so far away, my last breath would I pay for you to spend your life with me. I think of you each and every day. My life I would pay to spend with you each and every day. You're my heart and that I will never part for it streams life in every direction, therefore, son you carry my legacy into the next generation.

Next Dimension

My legacy is secure in my Children.

Certainties

One thing's for certain and two for sure in life there are no warranties but probabilities. So, destiny and perseverance comes into play as you attempt to make your dreams reality. The only guarantee in life and death is that you will harvest the rewards of your fate.

Next Dimension

Amen!

The Master of Irrelevance

You always have something to say even though your words don't pay, so my attention you don't sway. Your conversation is real slick that's how you get left behind real quick, as the master of irrelevance. I didn't make your rules but if you disrespect me I'll give you the blues. For nothing you say or do can change my interpretation of you.

Next Dimension

Sometimes you have to put people into circles that you control.

Masterpiece

I want to unleash my mind to this designed time
for the universe to explore, hopefully, all will
enjoy. As well as know how I flow with this pen
and pad about the love I've had and the storms of
life which were critical but developmental.
Nevertheless, the love I've exhibited was never
remorseful. Staying on course with the focus of
purpose as my only choice never paying any mind
about what's left behind, but pressing forward to
my projections and navigating in the right
direction.

Next Dimension

Staying focused on your purpose will bring
accomplishments.

Tomorrow about This Time

Tomorrow about this time God will have blessed me with another year on this earth. As I reflect there are many dreams I've yet to accomplish and a few goals that I have exceeded, for I have seen greatness as well as failure and they both worked towards my favor. So, I want to publicly praise God for what He's done also say hallelujah to what I've become and by the grace of God the Lord is not done with his son.

Next Dimension

Happy Birthday to 49 years on the earth

CT

A man of substance, whose core values are impeccable and love for his fellowman is incredible. You're still a young man in the developmental stages of emotions, nevertheless wisdom of an advanced age. So, turn the page on the things you've done, enhance the man you'll become and for that I say well done young man well done!!! Heal soon!

Next Dimension

Stay strong bro.

Mindset

I withstood all negative attacks and kept my manhood intact. They miscalculated my mindset thinking I'm uncouth and easily upset. That's not my style, my skill set is to figure out how with a smile. Like when they said I won't finish high school, "fools". I completed graduate school, and to those who said I couldn't get it done oh ye of little faith, I have 5 self-published books one by one.

Next Dimension

Do not let negativity overwhelm your gifts and abilities.

Mathematics

The calculations of infinity, the evaluator of intelligence, the designer of dimensions in creation, and the formula of eternity for she holds the theory's that produced earth. Never define with time for she designates destiny like second to none. Infinite in her approach, the quantifier of truth and all was defined when God gave birth to you!

Next Dimension

Mathematics, my first love

Growth

Pittsburgh, PA is where I jumped off the porch. Tuskegee, Alabama is where I initially showed no remorse for negativity but stayed on course towards productivity. I committed to my brand that's why I'll enhance and develop my body, mind, and health. Therefore, each day is a new beginning and with every breath I'm winning!

Next Dimension

Become a better person tomorrow than you were today.

An Eagle

I fly above negative connotations, disrespectful arrangements, deceitful lies, deceptive tears, and all fears.

Next Dimension

Take to the clouds when it comes to the aforementioned domains.

Color

Black is the color of your fear as well as the color of my dear for black is the color of my family and friends so how could it be the color of sin?
Black is the color of my skin and for that I'm condemned? I officially declare that I don't care no longer depressed, because validation is not yours to give for God gave me this life and I will live absent of historical lies, and present false alibis.

Next Dimension

Live your life.

Reality

When I was a young lad, people labeled me as a
fist fighter. When I got older they found out that
I'm an attentive writer, a publisher of my own
thoughts. From this point on I'll never let anyone
box me into their beliefs for my purpose is strong
and my legacy continues to infinity and beyond.
So reality is a component of my philosophy as well
as dreams, vision, and destiny.

Next Dimension

Be yourself!

Miscommunication

My vision is strong, and purpose is lifelong so your opinion of me is wrong. Nevertheless, I will never confront or put you in check, but let my character show, so all will know how I actually flow. Never frowns but always a smile turning that negativity upside down, so to that end don't take this personal my friend for integrity will always win.

Next Dimension

Your integrity will describe you.

Now versus then

My life has turned out right I gave up all the
negative behavior without a fight. Way back when
my life was a wreck equivalent to a bounced
check. I understood and acknowledged my faults
then; I put an assault on my purpose and
supplanted my brand, now I'm in high demand.
It's called reinventing yourself continuously and
that's what I do to shift from now versus then.

Next Dimension

Reinvent yourself continuously.

Ambiguous Man

Men of tone skin, second class citizens for they misunderstood his projected place in the human race, don't forget the pace for he would win an equal race. So continue to manipulate the mind, it's due to fear, but he'll catch you in time from behind. Just keep in mind his only unjust sin is the color of his skin. For they still sing freedom will ring for the dark skinned king.

Next Dimension

Hate for the color of skin is sin.

Options

Save me from myself, these options are not good for my health, please save me from myself for all I think about is stealing, concealing, and getting wealth. Save me from myself these options are too much for I need God's guiding touch.

Next Dimension

When you accept that you're doing evil that's the initial step to recovery.

Deliver me from me

I know you paid the price for my life and saved me from my own strife. I want to make your kingdom of pearly gates and streets paved with gold humbly my eternal home. So please deliver me from my self-effected sins and iniquities. Amen

Next Dimension

To God is the glory!

Grandma's Prayers

Grandma's prayers were never unanswered;
Grandma's prayers removed fear and ringed bells
in satan's hell. Saints came from miles around to
receive Grandma's Prayers released in the
atmosphere on their behalf. A true prayer warrior
in the army of God

Next Dimension

Grandma's legacy is within me.

Wise Counsel

Diverse in your approach exhibiting equivalence to most, giving educated advice for a misguided life, helping all navigate through trials of life. Yes, that's what wise counsel will do for all including me and you.

Next Dimension

Wise counsel is guided by God

Jokes on You

When you thought that goofy stuff was cool I was going to school, when you thought being in the streets acting a fool was cool I was finishing graduate school. Now you just completed a 10 year prison term and nowhere to call home so back to the streets you have to roam. Nevertheless, look back on your life, and now you see all the strife, just confess your sins, because with God you can always make amends.

Next Dimension

God will hear your cry.

Strange Fruit

The same strange fruit that overwhelmed my ancestors minds, the same strange fruit from death's vine, is the same complexion but in present times. The fallacy is how we could be foolish enough to take on the slave masters mentality and show your own this type of brutality. Yes, Willie Lynch played a part, nevertheless, now it's in your heart to kill others who look like your brother and cause pain to those who favor your mother. I hope you well, but with this mentality your home will be a prison cell and the next stop will be hell.

Next Dimension

Black on black crime is the strange fruit of our times.

Trusting you

A person is only dumb to the crude, stupidity exemplified by a fool. Therefore never dummy down for another but saturate them with your gifts as you reinforce greatness.

Next Dimension

All God's children are gifted.

My Gift

They ask why I write so freely, because the
creativity is inside of me. This favor is the way I
walk and talk so I could never have writers block.
For these are phases of my life I'm dividing with a
knife and putting samples on each page. So I hope
you engaged every stage of my plight and learn my
life.

Next Dimension

Transparency is healthy when you are pursuing
growth.

Gifted

I celebrate people individually for they're different from me, never trying to emulate them in any way, shape, or form. I enjoy each person's gifts for its granted from the Lord but it's up to each person individually to develop and enhance their abilities.

Next Dimension

All God's children have abilities so respect them as you respect your gifts.

Promiscuous Mind

You want to shake your behind, being sexy is always on your mind, social media is your custom room and that's where you get undressed more or less. Promiscuity is the times, it's not the bodies fault, but the mindset, eventually something you'll regret. Reframe from this life or death game for attention and fame and reclaim your integrity and the value of your name.

Next Dimension

Respect yourself.

Legacy

Look into your mind to define what you want to leave behind. Strive to demonstrate those characteristic each day also develop and enhance your brand so your character will endure guaranteed trials and tribulations. Then, a legacy of integrity will evolve from your brand.

Next Dimension

Your brand defines your legacy.

Human element

The good and bad, the happy and sad, the smiles and frowns, the tears and fears, the sunshine and the rain, the chains and the attempt to be free, it's all in me.

Next Dimension

Humanity is a step below angelic beings.

L. Ford

Through forgiveness comes repentance, through weakness comes strength, through perseverance comes confidence, through knowledge comes accountability, and through understanding come competence, through trials and tribulations comes purpose. Lifting the veil of ignorance is your sword being blessed by God is your reward therefore the ignorance will be exploited, love of self will be rewarded, resiliency is the approach, thus self-confidence will never be broached, so stay the course by lifting your voice and when life ends you will have no remorse.

Next Dimension

L. Ford is a good dude.

I made it?

You made it where by changing the texture of your hair, or the place you reside and what you drive? That's right keeping in stride with the dominating race and when injustice happens you frown and say "Those people are a disgrace to the humane race". Then, you quote Fox news because they justify these unjust rules. Remember your tone is natural man no need for a tan, your physical gifts and the way you run is second to none for your fearfully and wonderfully designed, so take those blinders of your mind.

Next Dimension

Be the best your God created.

Modern Gladiator

You want me to jump high, run swift then grin, but if I commit a sin you want to give me 5 to 10 in the pen. Promote me to the pinnacle as if it's the norm, as soon as I hit that peak you chop me down and remove my crown, go figure, this is the life and times of a modern day stud nigger. You love me when I run that ball, but don't let me walk with a Caucasian woman through the mall. I have seen it all!

Next Dimension

Please remember the stories from the past because they can be repeated.

Motivation

I'm motivated from pain and maximum gain, what can I say, this is the world in which I like to play. I write about spirituality, sexuality, reality, dreams, and fantasies. Nevertheless, I don't lie, shed tears, nor cry for living my life with empathy so no need for sympathy. I did my best with the life I was given, and to God I request wisdom for all the trials and tests.

Next Dimension

I love life and I live it free of fear.

Reinvent myself continuously

Another second, minute, hour, and day of reinventing myself continuously for I never let another's actions move me to the destructive range, but if they stay around my presence there will be a difference in them as well as a blessing for me.

Next Dimension

Be a blessing

Potential

Great is my fate, so I anticipate nothing less than the best test in life for to whom much is given much is required. It is essential for me to perfect my potential I give my best in everything I do and all that I pursue.

Next Dimension

Potential is essential if turned into purpose.

Don't judge me

I do whatever I want because God knows my heart so don't judge me for if you do then, you're my enemy therefore no friend to me. I stay high, lie, and falsify. I do what I please in God's eyes and say a couple scriptures to justify my indiscretions for my like-minded friends see my true religion. I only believe the parts of the bible that justifies my sin. Then, I cut the other scriptures out with a knife. No accountability is my life

Next Dimension

No accountability can last a lifetime but not an eternity.

Random thoughts

You swiped my life, minimize my plight, rape my wife, and then told me that this was right. Now my history is extorted then exported to a land of the red man that was usurped, and you said "it didn't hurt". You were so unkind when you infiltrated my mind and defined me as less than a man then stole and pillaged my native land. Nevertheless, after all of this you turn around and said reparation is a myth. There's no mystery that you misrepresented world history.

Next Dimension

The definition of pillage

When Love Hurts

This chapter is dedicated to the process of falling in and out of love.

Short Stories

These stories are focused on enhancing long-term inspiration and short-term stimulation as well as mind altering gratification. So take your time and please read each word one at a time, because there's wisdom in what is known as rhythm and rhymes. Please don't miss it nor get the message twisted. The knowledge is for you and you and especially you!

Next Dimension

A short story gives life to expressions.

Initial

It all starts off nice when we initially combined our lives. I became your husband and you my wife, a true love infused us together, we endured every forecast of weather, exploring our body types while making love every night with no exceptions we role played to keep us in the mood. Let's revisit that serenity and return that woman to me.

Next Dimension

Love should be renewed daily.

The Enemy in Bed

When a loved one inflicts grief, its equivalent to a great amount of hate saturating your fate for this experience is deep and will have tears creeping down your chin to no end. No need to be ashamed, but endure that pain for it's so hard to understand that hurt people can be evil. Nevertheless, life goes on and now you have the option to move on.

Next Dimension

Hurt people hurt people.

Why

Something happened along the way that transformed our affiliation into hate and now we no longer have the propensity to communicate. For goodness sake, can we revisit what's going on and the reason we're moving on in separate directions? It's been more than ten years of being soul-mates, are you willing to toss that away like we started this thing yesterday? Well, I'm willing to make corrections, but please no more rejections of my affections, for it's my hope that our love has a resurrection.

Next Dimension

Reconciliation is a good thing when it's mutual.

Bad Place

I pulled up to the bar like I was a so called star, sat next to another guy, but he had many drinks therefore he didn't think. He starts talking about a few female conquests one in particular had a rose tattooed on her chest and how she was a cutie with a phat booty. He went on to elaborate on how they made love in her house but the only problem was her spouse. Then, he describe this girls beauty and slipped up and said her name was Judy, also showed me a picture. To my surprise I almost made him cry, I think it was my 40 Cal poking him in the side for that was my wife and he was pleading for his life. I informed him there's no need to cry and give any alibis. I had him call her up and let her know what was said, she tried to deny the allegations and her participation but it was too late, because he gave detailed information like times and dates. So the last thing I told her was I never wanted to see her face, and I informed him that he will live but my marriage to Judy is dead.

Next Dimension

When you talk there are people who listen.

Pride within

At times I underestimate myself, undervaluing my sense of wealth, and put many demands on my plate for my only fear is to fail. So I give it my best to excel beyond my expectations hoping for validation through acclamation. I enjoy completing an assignment and getting a well done. I know its pride and I hope you understand and let it ride.

Next Dimension

Validation comes from the Lord.

This Isn't It

I know what love is and this isn't it. If cheating, stealing, and lying is love, then love has to repent. Those systemic issues have meticulously molded your so called love into a fraudulent image. So change your last name, because I'm discontinuing this game. Nevertheless, I showed you how to love. Hopefully, you learned but for us the bridge is burnt.

Next Dimension

Treat your spouse equal or better than you treat yourself.

Bye

I want to cry but I don't want you to know, so you
should just go for you hurt me and you're so
unkind I can't bare your touch. I loved you so, but
for my sanity I have to let you go. You took a
journey through my mind and left my body behind.
Therefore, I will no longer assign time to what you
left behind and that's my peace of mind

Next Dimension

If love hurts you have to identify the pain.

Perfect Timing

When your home is no longer your throne it's time to move on. When your best is rejected to the point of being disrespected it's time to move on. When you second guess yourself because of mental suppression, deception, lies, and depression it's time to say goodbye. Loving another shouldn't have to hurt or feel like double duty at work, but serenity from all enemies and wonderful bliss with your Mr. or Mrs. Discerning the season in a relationship is a wishful thing for we all have free will, therefore a forced romance is a unfortunate stance.

Next Dimension

A relationship is between two mutual parties.

Unravel

Our future is filled with gloom due to the things
you say and it's blue for what you refuse to do.
The lack of fulfilling my needs and all your wants
motivated by greed will continue to impede our
growth and inhibit this relationship's worth. So, I
concede you need a fool to fill your greed because
you go way beyond what I need.

Next Dimension

Greed will impede love in a relationship.

A House detached from a Home

We will never have a home if you continue to roam. This yin and yang is driving me insane for you proclaim that you're not into games, but you want others to call your name. Then you say you're with me but the following day your request is to be free. So baby, what's it going to be?

Next Dimension

Decide your priorities before getting into marriage.

Exceeded expectations

Hey Baby a slow process is better than no progress and all I have is what I provide. So, if you are demanding more get another venue because I can no longer serve you from my menu.

Next Dimension

When a person is giving their best, recognize the effort, and then evaluate your options.

So Long

Babe, I can hear it in your tone you want to be alone, I can see it in your eyes displaying goodbye, and I can feel it in our lack of intimacy that you're not feeling me. So I'll leave without disgrace and exit your space, nevertheless, there's no coming back for your assigned time is forever declined

Next Dimension

There is a time for love and there is a time for departure. It's your task to understand the seasons.

True Lies

Some people live not to die nevertheless, they croak inside, for fear overtakes their will and diminishes all their skills now they only have a dash of life. Therefore, don't be scared and denounce any fear then wipe it from your mind and demand that the source gets behind your conscious state of mind.

Next Dimension

Don't let fear live in your mind.

This isn't Love

Agony from my heart is tearing me apart for the
moves you make my heart breaks. It's my hope
that you go with every blow for its pain you
bestow on me, just set me free from all your lies
and inconsistencies. Yeah, I was hurt because of
what you put me through, nevertheless, that's life
and eventually, another's love I will pursue

Next Dimension

When pain is what you look forward too, then you
need another venue.

Closed Door

I love, but hesitate to like you; with all the things you do I can't even imagine spending my life with you. A queen of destroying joy, a rejecter of fun as far as an opened dialogue we have none. I hope we could be friends, because this intimate relationship has come to an end.

Next Dimension

There is a fine line between love and hate.

Yes

Baby, you're a pot of gold, but he treats you like your forming mold. I'm sure your current situation is getting old. Baby, put in your transfer and I'll give love untold, that will endure all that life has in store for us to explore. Sweetheart, walk and don't even talk and I'll pick you up down the block, leave with whatever is on your back and I will restore you and ensure that you're intact. You need a man that doesn't use his back hand to reinforce demands, but a man that's tender to the touch and loves you very much. So stick to the plans and get this love on demand.

Next Dimension

The grass is always greener from a distance.

Self-Gratification

If you don't want to love me, I'll make love to
myself. Nevertheless, I'm trying to share this
wealth. I will always be built up, I just hope you
could take it back down; it's identified as a
yearning so how does that sound? Nevertheless,
there's something in this for you coming once or
twice maybe even thrice. Trust me I will pay the
price, but you will enjoy the sacrifice

Next Dimension

If you can't get any support then do it yourself.

Your Fault

You were in the presence of greatness, but you didn't know how to fulfill your roll now you have to go. Sorry it was only one chance, because he is in high demand. Nevertheless it was a learning process even though you failed the test.

Next Dimension

You may have one chance in a lifetime for true love. Take advantage of your chance.

One Night Stand

Our initial meeting I thought we were going to
strategies like playing chess, but to my surprise
after a few words it turned into sex. Then, you
asked me what's next? I was perplexed so in a
hurry I left the scene. I know you thought that was
mean. You, gave you to me so soon, that a future
relationship with me was doomed, and because of
our start, I could never give you my heart. For I'm
not naive enough to think this is a one-time thing
therefore, sex will be our ultimate dream.

Next Dimension

Intimacy too soon will almost always resolve your
dream for marriage, commitment, and a ring.

Remorse

Baby I regret my debt of making you upset. I lost my job but I want it back, yes, you're making me sweat nevertheless, let's return to me making you wet. I know I did the crime therefore, my absence from you is the time. I want my life back because this situation is turning me blue as well as my body still yearns for you

Next Dimension

How do you ask for forgiveness?

Played Yourself

Now, when you call me on my cell phone all you get is a ringtone, begging me on your knees wanting sympathy saying forgive me please. But before you got caught you had no humility doing whatever you wanted to do with your number two. Well baby, the joke's on you.

Next Dimension

All things will come to an end.

Love to Hate

Why do you get mad with everything I say and do
except when it's done for you? Experts say get
away from you real soon, I'm going to take their
advice and put this relationship on ice, so stay cool
because you and I have always been about you.

Next Dimension

In a true relationship you have to commit a 100%.

Sincerely Yours

Your presence was a gift; our past persuaded me with an abundance of integrity. The only thing I regret is my incompetent and forcing you to say goodbye. Trust me I'm incomplete it's like a failed class I must complete. Please forgive me for I've lost and my love has paid the cost. I thank you for all that was gained please forgive me for any pain.

Next Dimension

A lost love still hurts when time has passed.

A Help Mate

Baby I don't know what to say because each time I talk my words get in the way. For goodness sake I put my confidence in you much too late therefore, this will be my fate. So, if you go away that's the price I'll have to pay, please understand you will be a game changer in my life as well as a rearrange of this fallacy that redefines my reality. Please help me become free from this negativity that's trying to control me.

Next Dimension

Sometimes you have to ask for what you need before it's granted.

Resigned

Well its true, so no fairy tale ending for you, our
vows are broke therefore, this love is revoked, 10
years given now its ending, and divorce pending.
No suggestions nor corrections, my only remorse
is that we couldn't stay on course. Please
remember I will always respect you, but because
of our current situation I have to reject you

Next Dimension

Good bye isn't necessarily the end.

Wait

There's a lot to explore for a girl and a boy if they grow and develop in life and become husband and wife. Then with life situations, a relationship may change and they want to give and get back their last name, therefore the decision you're ready make, please wait before it becomes your fate

Next Dimension

Get wise counsel

In My Heart

Is it love, like, lust, infatuation or mistrust, are you contemplating another's touch? Is it real, or did you ever care? Is it by design that we don't spend quality time? For the abundance of the heart will define your thoughts.

Next Dimension

Out of the abundance of the heart, the mouth speaks.

Go Your Way

A year ago we began, before the second year I
took a stand and said that's enough of your
disrespectful stuff. I'm leaving you because of your
jealousy, how could it be with all your insecurities
you had your whole family hating me. That's cool
you thought I was a fool, but you forgot that I'm
old school so I've seen your display a mile away,
please just go your way!

Next Dimension

Respect others gifts for jealousy leads to hate.

Lose time

Baby, I gave you the love of my life, but recently, I think I'm not all you have, it's clear that we don't share mutual cares. When we talk I don't sense any sympathy, nor empathy, but regret, and disdain. Now, I see the tears streaming from your eyes; nevertheless, the heart doesn't lie. I've given all my time, last dime; I even assigned to you my body and mind. I am requesting a refund because I'm presently done.

Next Dimension

Trust is the primary foundation in a relationship.

Homework

If you refuse to care for business at home but instead you prefer to trip, dip, and do a little bit of this and that, then your homework is undone. Sooner than later someone else will be having your fun. For you can make work at home delightful with some communication, instigation, and satisfaction.

Next Dimension

Make sure your home is secure and there will be no reason to explore.

The End

It's not my intention to have you sad or mad but negativity is all you mention when it comes to me. You say my jokes are jive I also take too much time working to keep us alive, as well as our relationship is wrong and you don't want to continue on with me. Therefore, if you don't see me as a gift I will gladly remove myself from this relationship. I believe deceit has a hold on you. Nothing I can say or do will change that boo. So, I will no longer waste your time I'm saying goodbye

Next Dimension

The End

Edgar A. Folks is a line and rhyme Philosopher, modern day poet of spoken-word, and lyricist. His writings are as diverse as he is, speaking to the hearts of lovers, young and old alike to make them wise at heart. His published books, **A Sample of Me, Affirmations 'The Inner-Most of a Man', Stimulus and Response, Teachable Moments 'The Cognitive Approach' and Rhythmic Expressions 'The Next Dimension'** are perfectly suited for use in plays, songs, spoken-word, and small group sessions, as well as for television and multi-media productions. Professionally, Edgar enjoys playing sports and developing himself spiritually. He earned a B.S. degree in Mathematics from the prestigious Tuskegee University, and a Master's Degree in the Art of Teaching from the University of Pittsburgh. Edgar has worked in the capacity of Teacher, Counselor, Therapist, and Advocate in support of enhancing and developing young people for over 25 years. Edgar resides in Pittsburgh, PA (USA).

Made in the USA
Middletown, DE
18 March 2016